The First Book of Broadway S[olos]

Compiled by Joan Frey Boytim

ISBN-13: 978-0-634-02281-4
ISBN-10: 0-634-02281-4

HAL•LEONARD®
CORPORATION

7777 W. BLUEMOUND RD. P.O. BOX 13819 MILWAUKEE, WI 53213

Visit Hal Leonard Online at
www.halleonard.com

Preface

When a beginning student of voice is ready for song literature, it is very important that some musical theatre material be included in the lesson repertoire. (This comment applies to American, Canadian, British, or other native English-speaking students.) Show tunes are a unique American and British contribution to the music world. Many of them are very useful for developing a smooth vocal line in an idiom that speaks to teenagers and new adult students. Not only is the music very melodic, the fact that the words are in a student's native language is an enormous advantage. *The First Book of Broadway Solos* attempts to address a traditional, classical voice teacher's sensibilities and needs in teaching basic techniques of singing.

The frustrations that I have experienced as a teacher are: (1) the vocal selection books from individual shows have, at most, two or three suitable songs for a particular voice; (2) the many piano/vocal show tune collections available have only several songs in good vocal study keys (mezzo-soprano being the exception); (3) the editions of songs taken from the actual vocal scores found in excellent publications such as *The Singer's Musical Theatre Anthology* are, in many cases, unsuitable for the beginning student because they are too long, too involved, and often in difficult keys for the novice singer.

The songs selected for *The First Book of Broadway Solos* were chosen for use by beginning voice students to assist in developing a solid vocal technique during the first several months or years of lessons. In most cases, the original voice category is preserved, although at times I chose, for musical and vocal reasons, to use a song originally sung by a baritone or tenor, for instance, in the mezzo-soprano collection (of course, taking into account the suitability of the text). Many keys have been altered to accommodate the ranges of the majority of teenagers and beginning adult students using these books. For those persons coming from a theatre point of view, it should be noted that these books are not designed for the belting style of singing. Specifically, mezzo-soprano is classically defined in this series (rather than the definition of this voice type by the theatre world as a belter). That is not to say that a more theatrical style of singing is not important or needed in other contexts. For the purposes of vocal instruction, classically based, lyric singing is the aim of this series.

Because many of the standard show tunes tend to be too low for the developing soprano voice, the majority of the keys in that volume have been raised. Most of the songs focus on a modest range comfortable for beginning singers, although several songs will showcase those students who are developing a higher vocal range. Many of the original keys, as published in the vocal selections of a show, were retained for the mezzo-soprano volume. More than half of the keys in the tenor collection have been raised to meet the vocal needs of the higher male voice. In most cases, the ranges in the baritone/bass volume have been lowered because the typical beginning baritone or bass struggles with the upper range tessitura and occasional high notes. A few of the songs were transposed down for the true bass range.

All the books include a few vocally challenging pieces, as well as a few more unfamiliar and unique entries. Overall, the songs in these four volumes include a wide variety of classics representative of the last seventy-five years of Broadway shows.

It is my hope that the studio voice teacher or the high school choral director will find this series a valuable resource, providing students with literature that is teachable, fun, and is an excellent introduction to the unique art form of musical theatre.

Joan Frey Boytim

The First Book of Broadway Solos

Compiled by Joan Frey Boytim

ALL THE THINGS YOU ARE

VERY WARM FOR MAY

Lyrics by OSCAR HAMMERSTEIN II
Music by JEROME KERN

AND THIS IS MY BELOVED
KISMET

Words and Music by ROBERT WRIGHT
and GEORGE FORREST
(Music Based on Themes of A. BORODIN)

10

CAN'T HELP LOVIN' DAT MAN
SHOW BOAT

Lyrics by OSCAR HAMMERSTEIN II
Music by JEROME KERN

his kiss - es got gin._____

Refrain (slowly)

Fish got to swim and birds got to fly,__ I got to love__ one

man till I die,__ Can't help lov - in' dat man__ of

mine._____ Tell me he's la - zy,

CLIMB EV'RY MOUNTAIN
THE SOUND OF MUSIC

Lyrics by OSCAR HAMMERSTEIN II
Music by RICHARD RODGERS

Maestoso

Refrain (*with deep feeling, like a prayer*)

Climb ev-'ry moun-tain, search high and low,

Fol-low ev-'ry by-way, ev-'ry path you know.

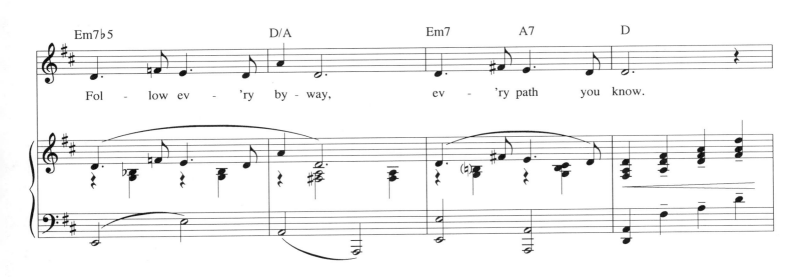

GOODNIGHT, MY SOMEONE

Meredith Willson's THE MUSIC MAN

Words and Music by
MEREDITH WILLSON

HELLO, YOUNG LOVERS

THE KING AND I

Lyrics by OSCAR HAMMERSTEIN II
Music by RICHARD RODGERS

Refrain *(Very moderately)*

star, Be brave and faith - ful and true _____

Cling ver - y close to each oth - er to - night I've been in

love like you. _____ I know how it feels to have

wings on your heels, And to fly down a street in a trance. _____

I COULD HAVE DANCED ALL NIGHT

MY FAIR LADY

Words by ALAN JAY LERNER
Music by FREDERICK LOEWE

I'LL KNOW
GUYS AND DOLLS

By FRANK LOESSER

Adapted as a solo here, the song is a
duet scene for Sarah and Sky in the show.

I HAVE DREAMED

THE KING AND I

Lyrics by OSCAR HAMMERSTEIN II
Music by RICHARD RODGERS

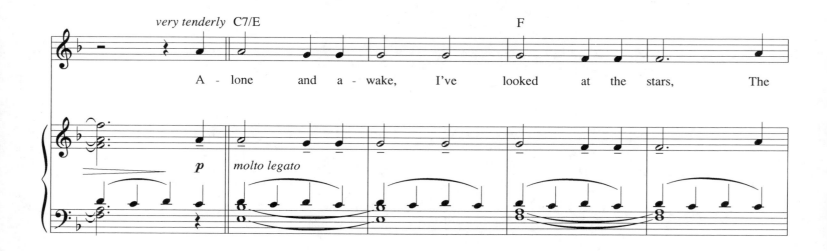

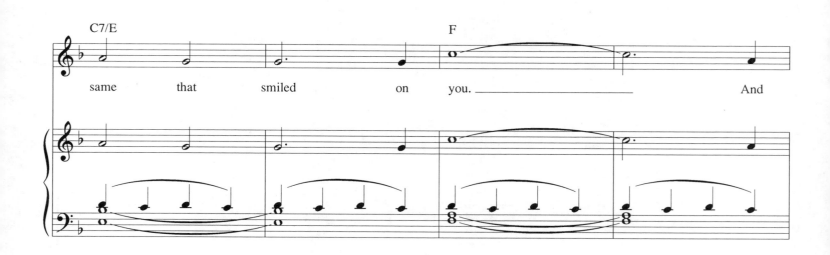

time and a - gain, I've thought all the things that
you were think - ing too.

Refrain (*slowly, with much expression*)

I have dreamed that your arms are love - ly

I have dreamed what a joy you'll be

C9 Gm7 C7 F A7
view In these dreams I've loved you so that by
mf passionately
Dm G7 F B♭ A7
now I think I know what it's like to be loved by
cresc.
Dm G9♭5 F Bdim B♭ C7
you I will love be - ing loved by
f
1 F C7
you.
p
2 F
you.
dim.
p

IT'S A GRAND NIGHT FOR SINGING
STATE FAIR

Lyrics by OSCAR HAMMERSTEIN II
Music by RICHARD RODGERS

It's a grand night for sing - ing! The moon is fly - ing high _____ And some-where a bird who is

41

43

JUST IMAGINE
GOOD NEWS

Words and Music by B.G. DeSYLVA,
LEW BROWN and RAY HENDERSON

REFRAIN

LOOK FOR THE SILVER LINING

SALLY

Words by BUDDY DeSYLVA
Music by JEROME KERN

LOOK TO THE RAINBOW

FINIAN'S RAINBOW

Words by E.Y. HARBURG
Music by BURTON LANE

Molto moderato

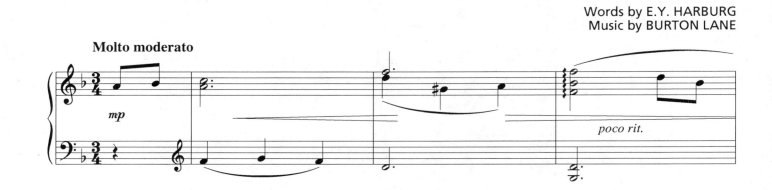

Very slowly (molto sostenuto)

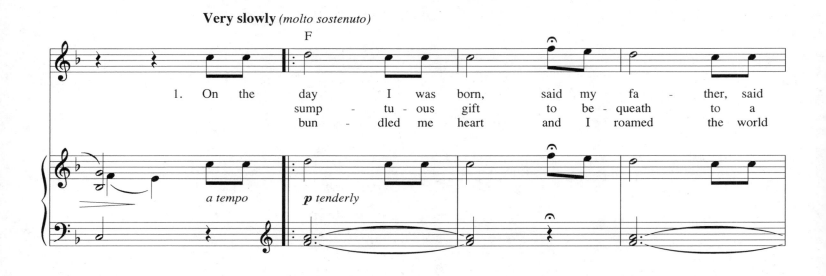

1. On the day I was born, said my fa - ther, said
sump - tu - ous gift to be - queath to a
bun - dled me heart and I roamed the world

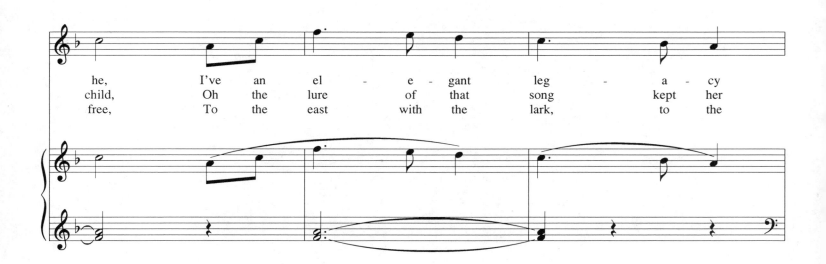

he, I've an el - e - gant leg - a - cy
child, Oh the lure of that song kept her
free, To the east with the lark, to the

54

THE SOUND OF MUSIC
THE SOUND OF MUSIC

Lyrics by OSCAR HAMMERSTEIN II
Music by RICHARD RODGERS

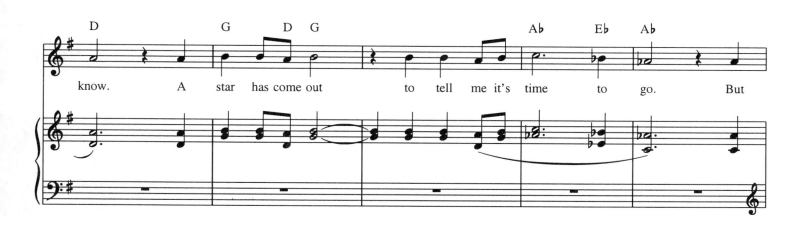

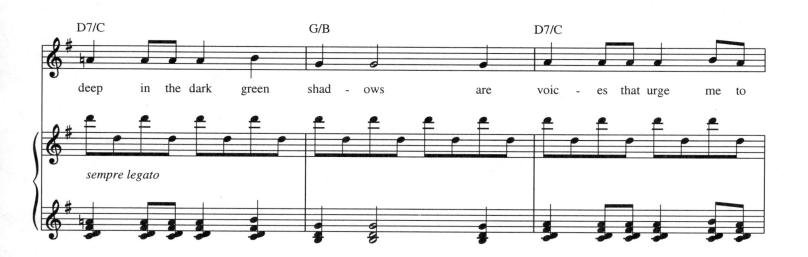

MAKE BELIEVE
SHOW BOAT

Lyrics by OSCAR HAMMERSTEIN II
Music by JEROME KERN

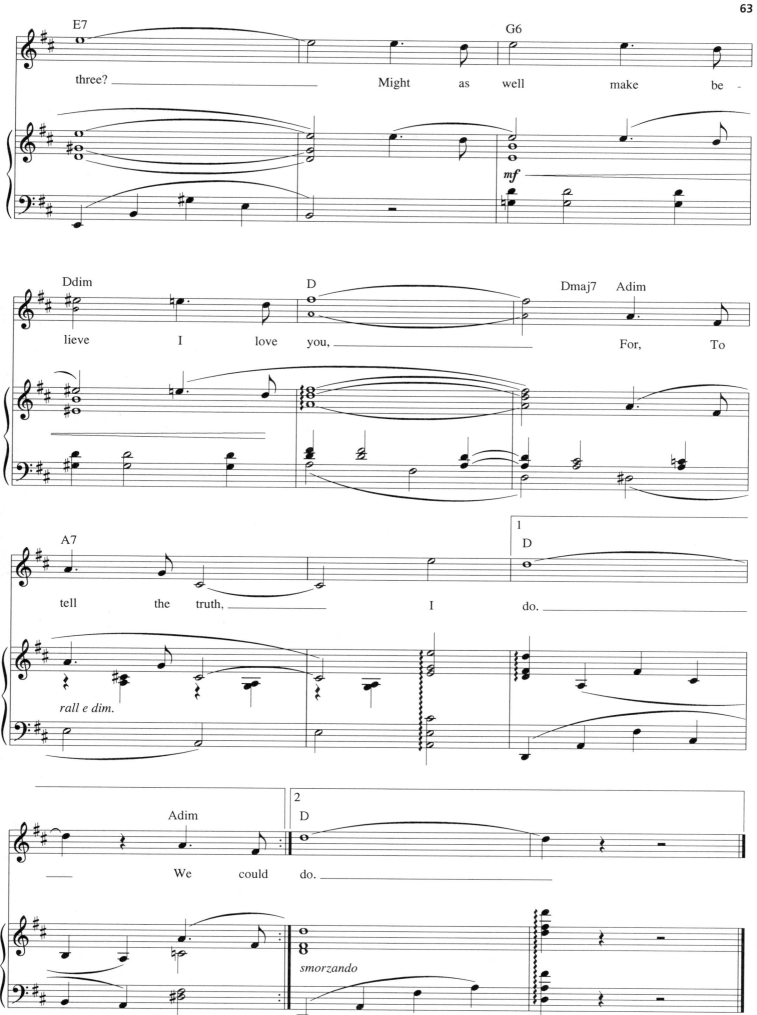

MANY A NEW DAY

OKLAHOMA!

Lyrics by OSCAR HAMMERSTEIN II
Music by RICHARD RODGERS

ONCE YOU LOSE YOUR HEART

ME AND MY GIRL

Words and Music by
NOEL GAY

OUT OF MY DREAMS

OKLAHOMA!

Lyrics by OSCAR HAMMERSTEIN II
Music by RICHARD RODGERS

THE SIMPLE JOYS OF MAIDENHOOD

CAMELOT

Words by ALAN JAY LERNER
Music by FREDERICK LOEWE

TILL THERE WAS YOU

Meredith Willson's THE MUSIC MAN

By MEREDITH WILLSON

WOULDN'T IT BE LOVERLY?
MY FAIR LADY

Words by ALAN JAY LERNER
Music by FREDERICK LOEWE

WHY DO I LOVE YOU?
SHOW BOAT

Lyrics by OSCAR HAMMERSTEIN II
Music by JEROME KERN

88

WITH A SONG IN MY HEART

SPRING IS HERE

Words by LORENZ HART
Music by RICHARD RODGERS

But it soon is a hymn to your grace. When the mu-sic swells

I'm touch-ing your hand; It tells that you're

stand-ing near, and At the sound of your

voice Heav-en op-ens its por-tals to me.

YOU'LL NEVER WALK ALONE

CAROUSEL

Lyrics by OSCAR HAMMERSTEIN II
Music by RICHARD RODGERS

Andantino molto cantabile

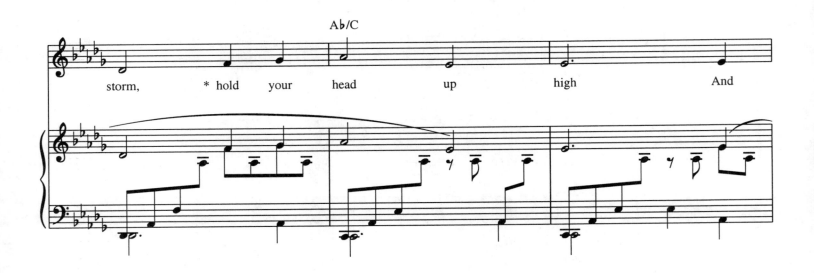

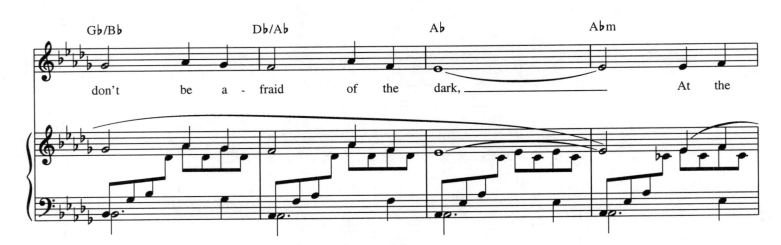

* alternate lyric: keep your chin up high